get ready go!

This is a book for

----

about starting
school.

You are starting school soon. How exciting!

You will be finding out about lots of new things,
and making new friends.

Get Ready Go! will help you to see what
school is like.

Schools are usually big buildings.

Some look old and some are
new – but they are all bright
and cheerful inside.

Remember, there will always be someone to help you at school, if you need it.

This little girl has lost her button. See if you can find the lost button on every page.

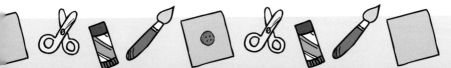

A teacher will look after you and help you learn at school.

Your teacher's name is

Draw a picture of your teacher here.

If there is anything you need to know at school, ask your teacher.

The teacher will have a register of names to check which children are in class today.

Kim

Darren

Ahmed

Darren

Ahmed

Kim

Sam

Is your name on this register?

If not, write it on the line.

Tick the names of the children who are here.

You will meet other grown-ups
at school as well as your class
teacher.
They are all there to help you.
There will be

a head teacher

a secretary

a caretaker

classroom and playground helpers

If you have to cross a busy road near your school, you might meet a lollipop person.
(But the lollipop isn't the kind you can eat!)

In your school,
these people's jobs may have different names.

At school, everything is specially for children. There will be toilets and washbasins just the right size for you.

You will need to wash your hands when you have been to the toilet.

There will be a place for you to
hang up your coat.

Write your name on the label and draw your
coat on the peg.

At school you will have lots of toys and books to share, and exciting things to do.

Finish what Ahmed has painted.

What do you think Kim and Darren are making?

Draw what Sam is pushing in her double buggy.

Draw the water pouring out of the jug.

It is usually best to leave your own toys at home, in case they get lost or broken.

Sometimes you will go into a big hall for an assembly with other children in your school.

It is a time when you can listen to a story together, sing a song and perhaps pray to God.

The grown-up at the front might have important things to say to everyone in the school.
Everyone walks quietly in and out of assembly.

You may have PE lessons where you can run and climb and jump.

After PE you will need to get yourself dressed again. Why don't you practise getting yourself dressed at home, so that you can manage by yourself at school?

Sometimes you will go into the playground to play. There might be lots of other boys and girls there.

Draw a ball for this girl.

Draw something for this boy to jump over.

Draw yourself playing with your friends.

If you haven't got anyone to play with, you can ask the grown-up in the playground to help you find a friend. Always tell them if you are worried about anything, too.

You might have a snack to eat during the morning, and something to drink.

orange juice

biscuit

apple

Colour in the apple. Draw some more fruit.

Perhaps you will have a school dinner or a packed lunch. Draw your favourite dinner.

Draw your favourite packed lunch.

If you are ever ill at school,
or you fall over and hurt
yourself, somebody will
look after you.

If you are really unwell, someone at school will
phone for your mum, dad or another grown-up
you know to take you home.

While you are busy at school, other people in your family will be doing different things. You may have brothers and sisters at school too, but what might the grown-ups be doing?

Tick the ones you think they might be doing while you are at school.

Can you say the days of the week?

Most children go to school every day except Saturday and Sunday. Colour in the days when you will go to school.

Sunday

Monday

Tuesday

Wednesday

Thursday

Friday

Saturday

Sometimes you won't go to school for a long time. There is usually a holiday at Easter, at Christmas and in the summer.

There are lots of things to learn at school. You will probably have a book to read at home.

Colour in the lollipops to match this number.

School is fun!

Now I go to school each day,
I've found that it can be
A very, very busy place,
That puts a smile upon my face –
Yes, school is fun for me.

Twice a week we do PE.
It's always such a treat.
We run and jump and skip
        and climb –
We really have a lovely time!
Yes, school's fun for my... feet.

My friends and I do paintings
On paper pegged on stands –
A red house, or a tall green tree,
A yellow boat, a bright blue sea.
Yes, school's fun for my... hands.

Sometimes we all sit quietly
And everybody hears
A funny tale in storytime,
Some lovely music, or a rhyme.
Yes, school's fun for my... ears.

Sometimes we do some cooking.
The things we make are yummy!
Chocolate crispies, sugar mice,
Fresh fruit salad – ooh, that's nice!
Yes, school's fun for my... tummy.

And all around our classroom
There are numbers, shapes
    and size,
And lots of lovely picture books,
And decorations hung from hooks –
Yes, school's fun for my... eyes.

At school I use my hands and feet,
My fingers, elbow, knee,
My eyes, my voice, my head, my toes,
My ears, my brain – so I suppose
School's fun for all of me!

Here is a prayer about school that you could say:

Dear God, please be with me as I start at school.
Thank you for all the people who will look after me
while I am there.
Help me as I learn new things and make new friends.
                      Amen

Writer: Marjory Francis
Artist: Helen Gale
Design: Mark Carpenter Design Consultants
Cover design: David Lund Design
Printed and bound by Belmont Press.

Thanks to the Road Safety Team, Milton Keynes for the loan
of the lollipop and uniform.

Look! I've found
my button!

Scripture Union, 207–209 Queensway, Bletchley, Milton Keynes MK2 2EB
www.scriptureunion.org.uk